From Aaron to Zipporah

Biblical NAMES *and their* MEANINGS

I0737513

ROSE PUBLISHING

Aaron (Bright/Light-bringer?)

אַהֲרוֹן ah-hah-ROHN

The name of Moses's brother and Israel's first high priest has an uncertain origin and meaning, but one possibility associates it with the Hebrew word for "light" (*or*). Ex. 4:14; 6:13; 7:7–12; 30:30; 32:1–5

Abel (Vapor/Breath)

הֶבֶל HEH-vehl

Throughout the Hebrew Scriptures, the name of Adam and Eve's second son is also used as a term describing the transitory, brief nature of life. This meaning connects well with Abel's early, tragic death at the hands of his brother, Cain. Gen. 4:1–10, 25

Abigail (My father's joy)

אֲבִיגַיִל ah-vee-GAH-yeel

One of King David's sisters and one of his wives have this name, which is based on two Hebrew words—one meaning "father" (*av*) and the other "to rejoice" (*gil*). 1 Sam. 25:3–42; 27:3; 2 Sam. 2:2–3; 3:2–3; 1 Chron. 2:13–17

Abraham (Father of a multitude)

אַבְרָהָם ahv-rah-HAHM

Although alternate views exist, the traditional view is that according to God's promise to make Abram ("exalted father") the "father of many nations" (Gen. 17:5), God changed his name to Abraham ("father of a multitude"). Gen. 12:1–3; 15:1–6; 17:1–8; 18:1–33; 22:1–14

Adam (Man)

אָדָם ah-DAHM

Adam's name fittingly describes how God created him: It is related to the word meaning "red/ruddy," like the color of skin or dirt, and is derived from *adamah* ("ground"). Another related word, *dam*, means "blood." Gen. 2:20–4:2, 25; 5:1–5

Amos (Burdensome/Burden-bearer)

עָמוֹס ah-MOHS

The verb related to this name (*amas*) means "to carry/bear a load." The word is common, but only the prophet Amos carries this name in the Old Testament. He carried the burden of God's contempt for the Northern Kingdom's sins. Amos 1:1; 7:10–15; 8:1–2

Andrew (Manly/Courageous)

Ἀνδρέας an-DRAY-as

Āner ("man") is the Greek root word for this name of one of Jesus's courageous disciples. Matt. 4:18–20; Mark 13:3–4; John 1:40–42; 6:8; 12:20–22

Asher (Happy/Fortunate)

אָשֵׁר ah-SHAYR

This name aptly describes the joy Asher's birth brought to Jacob's wife Leah. She hoped that bearing another son for Jacob (through her servant, Zilpah) would increase his affection toward her. Gen. 30:12–13; 35:26; 49:1, 20; Deut. 33:1, 24–25; Josh. 19:24–31

Barnabas
(Son of encouragement)

Βαρναβᾶς bar-nah-BAS

This Aramaic nickname of one of Paul's coworkers (originally called Joseph) literally means "one of the prophets/son of the prophets." Since prophecy can function as a means of encouragement, it is an apt description of Barnabas's ability to encourage and exhort others. Acts 4:32–37; 11:19–30; 13:1–3; 15:36–40

Bartholomew (Son of Talmai)

Βαρθολομαῖος bar-tho-lo-MAI-os

The name of this disciple is an Aramaic patronymic, meaning it is derived from a father or ancestor whose name in Hebrew means "plowman." It could be Bartholomew's surname, since many scholars believe he is the same man as the apostle Nathanael, who is mentioned only in the Gospel of John, where Bartholomew is not listed as an apostle. Matt. 10:2–3; Mark 3:13–19; Luke 6:12–16; Acts 1:12–13

Bathsheba
(Daughter of an oath/seven)

בַּת-שֶׁבַע baht-SHEH-vah

In Hebrew, "oath" is related to the word for "seven" (*sheva*), offering parallel meanings for the name of the wife of Uriah and later King David. The number seven symbolizes perfection/completeness, which relates to an oath as a complete and binding commitment. 2 Sam. 11:1–12:25; 1 Kings 1:11–31

Benjamin (Son of my right hand)

בִּנְיָמִין bean-yah-MEEN

After a difficult delivery, Rachel named her second son Ben-Oni ("son of my sorrow") right before she died; but Jacob renamed him Benjamin ("son of my right hand"). The right hand was a symbol of strength, skill, authority, and favor. Gen. 35:16–18; 42:1–43:34; 49:1, 27; Deut. 33:1, 12; Josh. 18:11–28

Boaz (In strength)

בֹּעַז BOH-ahz

As a wealthy, righteous landowner, Boaz led with moral strength and generously blessed those around him. King Solomon, a descendant of Boaz, used this name for the north pillar that supported the temple. Ruth 2:1–3:15; 4:1–13, 18–22; 1 Kings 7:21

Cain (Possession)

קַיִן KAH-yeen

At Cain's birth, Eve announced she had brought forth, or acquired, a man with the Lord's help. His name is a play on the word *qanah* ("to possess/acquire"). Gen. 4:1–17

Caleb (Dog)

כָּלֵב kah-LAYV

From the word for "dog," *kelev*. Characteristic of a dog's temperament, this name often represents faithfulness, wholeheartedness, and strength. Unlike most of Israel, Caleb wholeheartedly trusted God's promise that the Israelites could conquer the giants living in the promised land. Num. 13:1–14:38; 32:11–13; 34:16–19; Josh. 14:6–14; 15:13–19

Timothy
(Honored by God/Honoring God)

Τιμόθεος tee-MO-theh-os

A common Greek name that combines *timē* ("honor/reverence") and *theos* ("God"). Timothy, a disciple of the apostle Paul, both honored God and was honored by him. Acts 16:1–5; 17:14–15; 1 Cor. 4:14–17; 16:10–11; 1 Tim. 1:2–4

Titus (Nurse?)

Τίτος TEE-tos

This gentile coworker of Paul had a Roman name. The meaning is uncertain, but some have suggested "nurse" because of Titus's role in helping Paul establish and nurture churches. 2 Cor. 7:5–15; 8:16–24; 12:14–21; Gal. 2:1–5; Titus 1:4–5

Zacchaeus (Pure)

Ζακχαῖος zak-KAI-os

This chief tax collector's name is a Greek form of the Hebrew name Zakkai (from *zakhakh*, "to be pure"). When Zacchaeus encountered Jesus, he promised to give half his possessions to the poor and repay those he had cheated. Luke 19:1–10

Zebulun (Honor)

זְבֻלוּן zuh-voo-LOON

This name reflects Leah's declaration that Jacob would "honor" (*zaval*) her for bearing him six sons, symbolizing her desire for recognition and respect. Gen. 30:19–20; 49:1, 13; Ex. 1:1–4; Deut. 33:1, 18; Josh. 19:10–16

Zechariah
(The Lord remembers)

זְכַרְיָה zuh-khar-YAH

Ζαχαρίας zah-khah-REE-as

More than thirty people in the Bible bear this name. It was especially popular after the Jewish exile—an appropriate reminder that God had "remembered" (root: *zakhar*) his people in Babylon. Ezra 5:1–2; 6:14; 8:15–17; Neh. 8:4–5; Zech. 1:1; Luke 1:5–25

Zephaniah
(The Lord has hidden)

צְפַנְיָה tsuh-fahn-YAH

From the root word *tsafan* ("to hide/to treasure"), a term that is sometimes used to describe how the Lord keeps his treasured ones from harm. Jer. 21:1–2; 29:24–32; 37:1–3; Zeph. 1:1; Zech. 6:9–14

Zipporah (Bird)

צִפֹּרָה tseep-poh-RAH

The name of Moses's wife is based on a Hebrew word for "bird" (*tsipor*). Its root (*tsaphar*) can mean "to chirp/to dance/to leap." Ex. 2:15–22; 4:21–26; 18:1–6

Samuel
(Heard by God/Name of God)

שְׁמוּאֵל shuh-moo-AYL

The name of this prophet and judge combines the word for "to hear" (*shama*) or "name" (*shem*) with the generic Hebrew term for "God" (*El*). "Hear" indicates a play on Samuel's mother's declaration that God had heard and granted her request for a child. 1 Sam. 1:1–20; 3:1–21; 9:15–10:25; 16:1–13

Sarah (Princess)

שָׂרָה sah-RAH

Abraham's wife was originally known as Sarai before God renamed her Sarah. Both names could possibly mean "princess," with Sarai having foreign or pagan origins that were no longer fitting. Regardless, the change to Sarah indicated that God would make her a royal mother of nations and that kings would descend from her. Gen. 17:15–21; 18:1–15; 21:1–7; 23:1–2

Saul (Asked for)

שָׁאוּל shah-OOL

Derived from *sha'al* ("to ask"). Saul became the first king of Israel after the nation asked God for a king. 1 Sam. 9:1–2; 10:17–27; 15:1–35; 19:1–24; 24:1–22

Seth (Granted/Appointed)

שֵׁת shayt

When Eve gave birth to her third son, she called him Seth (from *shith*, "to appoint/grant") because God had granted her another child after Cain murdered Abel. Gen. 4:25–5:8; 1 Chron. 1:1–2

Simeon (Heard/One who hears)

שִׁמְעוֹן sheem-OHN

Συμεών soo-meh-OHN

Leah named her second-born child Simeon because she believed God "heard" (*shama*) that she was unloved by Jacob, and he compassionately responded by giving her another son. The Greek form is also transliterated as Simeon, with Simon as a variation. Gen. 29:33; 34:1–31; 49:1, 5–7; Matt. 10:1–4; Luke 2:22–35

Solomon (Peaceable)

שְׁלֹמֹה shuh-loh-MOH

After David's first son with Bathsheba died, God promised David that he would have a son named Solomon (from *shalom*, "peace") and that under his reign, Israel would experience peace. At Solomon's birth, the Lord sent word that he should also be called Jedidiah ("loved by the LORD"), but it is the only time that name is used in Scripture. 2 Sam. 12:24–25; 1 Kings 4:21–34; 11:1–43; 1 Chron. 22:5–19

Stephen (Crown)

Στέφανος STEF-an-os

Known as the first Christian martyr, Stephen performed great wonders and signs and boldly preached the gospel. Fitting to his name, a crown is promised to those who endure persecution, even to the point of death (Rev. 2:10). Acts 6:1–8:2; 22:1–5, 17–20

Thomas (Twin)

Θωμᾶς thō-MAHS

From the Aramaic word meaning "twin." The disciple Thomas was also known by the name Didymus ("twin" in Greek). Luke 6:13–16; John 11:11–16; 14:1–6; 20:19–29; Acts 1:12–14

Dan (Judge)

דָּן dahn

In Rachel's childbearing competition with Leah, she was at first infertile. As a solution, she gave her servant, Bilhah, to Jacob as another wife. With Dan's birth through Bilhah, Rachel believed God had "judged" (from the root word *din*) and vindicated her. Gen. 30:1–6; 49:1, 16–18; Ex. 1:1–5; Deut. 33:1, 22; Josh. 19:40–48

Daniel (God is my judge/Judge of God)

דָּנִיֵּאל dah-nee-YAYL

During the Jewish exile, Daniel was deported to Babylon and named Belteshazzar ("Bel protects his life"). Bel was the title of the Babylonian god Marduk, yet Daniel stayed loyal to the one true God while advising foreign kings. When he was thrown into a lions' den for refusing to pray to the king, "God (*El*) judged (from the root word *din*) in Daniel's favor" and sealed the lions' mouths. Dan. 1:1–21; 2:1–49; 4:4–27; 5:1–29; 6:1–28

David (Beloved)

דָּוִד dah-VEED

From the word *dod* ("beloved"). Known as a man after God's own heart, God regarded David as beloved in his sight, appointing him as Israel's second king and establishing the messianic line of Jesus through his descendants. 1 Sam. 16:11–13; 17:12–58; 2 Sam. 5:3–5; 7:1–17; Ps. 51:1–19

Deborah (Honeybee)

דְּבוֹרָה duh-voh-RAH

Deborah fearlessly served Israel as a judge and prophet. Some suggest that her name represents leadership, wisdom, and industriousness—traits shared with the honeybee, the literal meaning of her name. Also the name of Rebekah's nurse. Gen. 35:8; Judg. 4:1–15, 23–5:31

Eleazar (God has helped)

אֶלְעָזָר ehl-ah-ZAHR

Aaron's third son, who became high priest after Aaron's death. This name combines the words *El* ("God") and *azar* ("to help"). God helped Eleazar as he played a significant role during the conquest of the promised land. Many other biblical figures bear this name, sometimes with varied spellings. Gen. 15:1–2; Ex. 28:1; Num. 27:18–23; 1 Chron. 23:15; Neh. 12:40–42

Elijah (The Lord is God)

אֵלִיָּה ay-lee-YAH

Combines the generic Hebrew word for "God" (*El*) and the shortened form of God's personal name (*Yah*). This prophet's name is fitting because he opposed worship of the false god Baal and demonstrated the Lord's supremacy. 1 Kings 17:1–19:16; 2 Kings 2:1–11; Mal. 4:5

Elisha (God is salvation)

אֱלִישָׁע eh-lee-SHAH

Elisha served Israel's national leaders and performed miracles that demonstrated "God's (*El*'s) saving power (root: *yasha*)." Elisha's name also reflects God's miraculous deliverance when enemy troops pursued him. 1 Kings 19:13–21; 2 Kings 2:13–22; 4:1–37; 6:8–23; 13:14–21

Paul (Little/Small)

Παῦλος POW-los

The apostle Paul was originally known by his Hebrew name, Saul, but he used his Roman name, Paul, when he began his ministry among gentiles. It was common at the time for Jews to have both a Hebrew and Roman name. Acts 13:1–12; 19:1–41; 21:17–26; 28:11–31; Rom. 1:1

Peter (Rock/stone)

Πέτρος PET-ros

When Simon proclaimed that Jesus was Israel's promised Messiah, Jesus gave him the Greek name Peter (Cephas in Aramaic), signifying the future foundational role he would play in the church. Matt. 16:13–19; John 21:1–19; Acts 3:1–26; 10:24–48; 1 Pet. 1:1–2

Philip (Lover of horses)

Φίλιππος FIL-ip-pos

New Testament bearers of this name include Philip the tetrarch, the apostle, and the evangelist. It combines two Greek root words: *philos* ("love") and *hippos* ("horse"). The name often implied nobleness or leadership. Luke 3:1–3; John 1:43–48; Acts 1:12–13; 6:1–5; 8:26–40

Rachel (Ewe, a female sheep)

רָחֵל rah-KHAYL

Rachel's name fits her early beginnings as a shepherd. Jacob met Rachel at a well while she was caring for her father's sheep. She became his wife, but only after Jacob was deceived into first marrying Rachel's older sister, Leah. Gen. 29:1–31; 30:1–8, 22–24; 35:16–20; 48:7; Ruth 4:9–11

Rahab (Broad/Wide)

רָחָב rah-KHAHV

This Canaanite prostitute protected the two Israelites who came to spy on Jericho. Her name also functions as an adjective throughout the Hebrew Scriptures. Josh. 2:1–21; 6:16–25

Rebekah (Tied up/Secured)

רִבְקָה reev-KAH

Isaac's wife's name likely originates from an Arabic term referring to a rope used to tie animals. Figuratively, it may suggest a woman who "ensnares" or captivates men with her beauty, or the concept of securing that which is valuable. Gen. 24:1–67; 25:19–24; 27:5–17, 42–46; 49:29–31

Reuben (See, a son)

רְאוּבֵן ruh-oo-VAYN

The name of Leah's firstborn son combines words that mean "Look (*r'u*), a son (*ben*)." They also share a similar meaning to Leah's statement that the Lord had seen her misery of feeling unloved by Jacob. Gen. 29:31–32; 37:12–35; 49:1–4; Deut. 33:1, 6; Josh. 13:15–23

Ruth (Friend/friendship)

רוּת root

Ruth lived up to her name by showing her mother-in-law, Naomi, unwavering devotion and by pledging to remain with her until death. Ruth 1:1–3:18; 4:13–17

Samson (Sun-man/Sunny)

שִׁמְשׁוֹן sheem-SHOHN

The name of this strong and powerful judge of Israel is derived from the word meaning "sun" (*shemesh*). Judg. 13:2–16:30

Elizabeth (God is my oath)

Ἐλισάβετ eh-lee-SAH-bet

The Greek form of the Hebrew name Elisheba. Elisheba was the wife of Aaron the high priest; her name combines "God" (*El*) and "oath" (*sheva*). God enabled Elizabeth, a descendant of Aaron, to give birth to John the Baptist in her old age. Luke 1:5–45, 56–66

Ephraim (Double fruitfulness)

אֶפְרַיִם ehf-RAH-yeem

The name of Joseph's second son reflects how abundantly God had blessed Joseph in Egypt. Jacob adopted Joseph's sons as his own and blessed Ephraim with his right hand, foreshadowing the fruitful prominence Ephraim's descendants would have. Gen. 41:50–52; 48:1–20; Deut. 33:1, 13–17; Josh. 16:5–10; 17:14–18

Esau (Hairy?)

עֵשָׂו ay-SAHV

The meaning is uncertain, but Esau shares some sounds with the word for "hairy," matching his description at birth. Esau was also called Edom ("red") because he exchanged his birthright for red stew. Gen. 25:21–34; 27:1–41; 33:1–16; 36:1–8; Amos 1:11

Esther (Star?)

אֶסְתֵּר ehs-TAYR

Likely from the Persian word for "star." Queen Esther was originally known by the Hebrew name Hadassah ("myrtle"), but she kept her Jewish identity hidden until she knew she must plead with the king to save her fellow Jews. Est. 2:7–20; 4:1–5:8; 7:1–8; 9:20–32

Eve (Life-giver)

חַוָּה khah-VAH

Adam gave his wife a name that reflected her destiny as the mother of all people who would live on earth. Its root (*khayah*) means "to live." Gen. 3:20–4:2, 25

Ezekiel (God strengthens)

יְחֶזְקֵאל yuh-khehz-KAYL

From the verb *khazaq* ("to strengthen"), combined with *El* ("God"). God's hand strengthened Ezekiel as he spoke a message of repentance and the future restoration of God's people. Ezek. 1:1–3; 24:15–27; 37:1–28

Ezra (Help)

עֶזְרָא ehz-RAH

A shortened form of Azariah, meaning "God is a help." With God's help, Ezra the priest left Babylon to teach God's laws to the Jewish exiles returning to Jerusalem. Ezra 7:1–28; 9:13–10:17; Neh. 7:73–8:18

Gabriel (Man/Warrior of God)

גַּבְרִיאֵל gahv-ree-AYL

Γαβριήλ gah-bree-AYL

This archangel's name fits his role as God's messenger, bearing powerful messages. He explained to Daniel the meaning of his visions and announced the forthcoming world-changing births of John the Baptist and Jesus. Dan. 8:15–26; 9:20–27; Luke 1:5–38

Nahum (Comfort)

נַחוּם nah-KHOOM

A short form of Nehemiah, derived from *nakham* ("to comfort"). This prophet spoke comfort to God's people, announcing God's coming judgment against Nineveh, capital of Assyria, which had oppressed Judah for decades. Nah. 1:1–2:2

Naomi (My delight/pleasant one)

נָעֳמִי nah-oh-MEE

From *noam* ("pleasantness/sweetness"). After the death of her husband and two sons, Naomi urged the women of Bethlehem to call her Mara ("bitter") because she believed God had caused her to suffer. Ruth 1:1–21; 2:18–22; 3:1–5; 4:13–17

Naphtali (My struggle/my wrestling)

נַפְתָּלִי nahf-tah-LEE

Naphtali was Rachel's second son through her surrogate, Bilhah. At his birth, Rachel proclaimed that she had "won the struggle" with Leah for Jacob's affection. Leah had already given birth to four of Jacob's sons. Gen. 30:7–8; 35:25; 49:1, 21; Deut. 33:1, 23; Josh. 19:32–39

Nathanael (God has given)

Ναθαναήλ nath-an-ah-AYL

The Greek form of the Hebrew name Nethanel (from *nathan*, "to give," and *El*, "God"). Nathanael is mentioned only in the Gospel of John; many scholars identify him as the apostle Bartholomew mentioned only in the other Gospels. John 1:45–51; 21:1–14

Nehemiah (The Lord comforts)

נְחֶמְיָה nuh-khem-YAH

A combination of *nakham* ("comfort") and *Yah*, the shortened form of God's personal name. Nehemiah represented his name well as he helped rebuild Jerusalem after the Babylonian exile. Neh. 1:1–2:20; 7:6–7; 8:9

Nicodemus (Victorious among the people)

Νικόδημος nik-OD-ay-mos

Nicodemus, a member of the Jewish religious council, became a secret follower of Jesus. His Greek name was common among Jews and gentiles and derives from *nikos* ("victory") and *dēmos* ("people"). John 3:1–15; 7:37–52; 19:38–40

Noah (Rest)

נֹחַ NOH-ahkh

Similar to a word meaning "rest" (*nuakh*). Noah's father hoped his new son would bring people rest from God's curse on the ground. After the flood, Noah made sacrifices to the Lord, and they pleased him so much that God promised to never curse the ground again. Gen. 5:28–32; 6:5–9:29; Isa. 54:7–9; Ezek. 14:19–20

Obadiah (Servant of the Lord)

עֹבַדְיָה oh-vahd-YAH

More than ten men in the Old Testament bear this name. It combines the root word meaning "to serve" (*avad*) with the shortened form of God's personal name (*Yah*). The most well-known is the prophet Obadiah, who pronounced God's judgment against the nation of Edom.
1 Kings 18:1–15; 2 Chron. 34:12–13; Neh. 12:24–26
Obad. 1:1–21

Gad (Good fortune)

גָּד gahd

After birthing four sons for Jacob, Leah was no longer conceiving, so she gave her servant, Zilpah, to Jacob as a surrogate. Leah named Zilpah's first son Gad, reflecting her belief that "good fortune" (*gad*) had come in her quest to be loved by Jacob. Gen. 30:9–11; 35:26; 49:1, 19; Deut. 33:1, 20–21; Josh. 13:24–28

Gideon (Hewer)

גִּדְעוֹן geed-OHN

The root word (*gada*) means "to hew/cut down" and is often used to describe the destruction of idols. Gideon courageously cut down his father's idols and struck down the oppressive Midianites. Judg. 6:1–8:35

Goliath (Exile?)

גָּלְיָת gohl-YAHT

This Philistine champion's name may derive from a word that means "to uncover/remove" (*galah*) and can imply the humiliation of exile. 1 Sam. 17:1–54; 21:8–10; 22:6–10

Habakkuk (Embrace)

חֲבַקּוּק khah-vahk-KOOK

This prophet asked God why he had not responded to cries for justice amid Judah's wickedness. His name is derived from the word *khavaq* ("to embrace"). Hab. 1:1; 3:1

Haggai (Festive)

חַגַּי khahg-GAIY

Possibly a shortened form of Haggiah, which means "festival (*khag*) of the Lord (*Yah*)." Haggai was the first to prophesy after the Babylonian exile, encouraging God's people to rebuild the temple. Ezra 5:1; Hag. 1:1–2:23

Hannah (Grace)

חַנָּה khahn-NAH

From the word meaning "to show grace/favor/mercy" (*khanan*). The story of Hannah, the prophet Samuel's mother, is filled with examples of grace. Anna, who prophesied over the infant Jesus (Luke 2:36–38), has a Greek form of this Hebrew name. 1 Sam. 1:1–2:10, 18–21

Isaac (He laughs)

יִצְחָק yeets-KHAHK

From *tsakhaq*, "to laugh." In their old age, God promised Abraham and Sarah a son named Isaac. They laughed in disbelief, but after his miraculous birth, they laughed with joy.
Gen. 17:1–22; 18:1–15; 21:1–7; 22:1–14; 26:1–32

Isaiah (Salvation of the Lord)

יְשַׁעְיָהוּ yuh-shah-YAH-hoo

This prophet foretold not only the coming judgment and exile of God's people, but also how the "Lord" (*Yah*) would ultimately "save" (*yasha*) them by his gracious hand. Isa. 1:1; 2:1; 7:1–17; 38:1–8; 39:1–8

Ishmael (God hears)

יִשְׁמָעֵאל yeesh-mah-AYL

Combines the words for "God" (*El*) and "to hear" (*shamah*). Ishmael's name reflects the hardship his mother, Hagar, endured during her pregnancy. God heard of her distress and promised Hagar he would make Ishmael a great nation. Gen. 16:1–17:20; 21:1–21; 25:7–18; 28:6–9

Issachar (He will bring a reward)

יִשָּׂשכָר yee-sah-KHAR

From *sakhar* ("reward"). Amid Leah and Rachel's rivalry to bear children for Jacob, Leah declared at Issachar's birth that God had rewarded her for previously giving her servant, Zilpah, to Jacob as a childbearing surrogate. Gen. 30:9–18; 35:23; 49:1, 14–15; Deut. 33:1, 18–19; Josh. 19:17–23

Jacob (He grabs by the heel)

יַעֲקֹב yah-ah-KOHV

Born grasping his twin brother Esau's heel, Jacob's name is a play on the word *aqav* ("to grab by the heel"). It figuratively means "to supplant," which played out when the famished Esau asked Jacob for stew he had made. Jacob asked for Esau's birthright in exchange, and then he deceived their father to obtain Esau's firstborn blessing. After Jacob's wrestling match with God, God changed his name to Israel ("he struggles with God"). Gen. 25:19–34; 27:1–35:29; 37:1–10; 42:1–50:14

James (Supplanter)

Ἰάκωβος ee-AK-oh-bos

Derives from the Hebrew name Jacob. Two of Jesus's disciples and one of his brothers were named James. This brother went from being an unbeliever to an important leader in the early church. Matt. 4:21–22; 10:2–4; Mark 6:3; John 7:1–5; James 1:1

Jeremiah (The Lord will exalt/arise)

יִרְמְיָה yeer-muh-YAH

This common biblical name combines the word *rum* ("to rise/be exalted") and *Yah*, a shortened form of God's personal name, *Yahweh*. The book of Jeremiah powerfully represents the meaning of this name. Jer. 1:1–10; 18:1–12; 37:1–38:29; 40:1–6; Dan. 9:2

Jesus (The Lord saves)

Ἰησοῦς ee-ay-SOOCE

The Greek form of the Hebrew name Joshua (often shortened to Yeshua), which means "The Lord (*Yahweh*) saves (root: *yasha*)." Mary was commanded to name her first son Jesus because he would save people from the penalty of sin. Because this name was common, Jesus was often called Jesus of Nazareth. Later he was known as Jesus Christ, meaning Jesus the Messiah, or Jesus the Anointed One. Matt. 1:18–25; 27:35–37; John 1:29–34; Acts 2:36–38; Rom. 8:1–2

Jezebel (Where is the prince?)

אִיזֶבֶל ee-ZEH-vehl

This wicked queen led Israel to worship the idols Baal and Asherah. The meaning of her name is uncertain, but suggestions include "Baal exalts," "unexalted," and "unmarried." A more recent theory is that the Phoenician origin of her name could mean "Where is the prince [Baal]?"—a cry from Baal's worshipers during ritual ceremonies. 1 Kings 16:30–31; 18:4–19; 19:1–2; 21:4–25; 2 Kings 9:30–37

Martha (Mistress)

Μάρθα MAR-thah

This name likely comes from the Aramaic word for "mistress," in the sense of authority and ownership. Martha, a friend of Jesus, is known for her hospitality. Luke 10:38–42; John 11:1–44; 12:1–2

Mary (Beloved? Bitter/rebellious? Drop of the sea?)

Μαρία mar-EE-ah

Mary is the anglicized version of the Greek name Maria, which is transliterated from the Hebrew name Miriam. It may mean "beloved" if it has Egyptian origins. One Hebrew meaning derives from *meri* ("bitterness/rebellion") and another from *mar* ("drop") and *yam* ("sea"). Mary was the most common name for Jewish women in the first century, including the beloved mother of Jesus. Luke 1:26–38; 10:38–42; Mark 15:40–41; Acts 12:11–12

Matthew (Gift of the Lord)

Μαθθαῖος mat-THAI-os

An abbreviated Greek form of the Hebrew name Mattityah, meaning "gift (*matat*) of the Lord (*Yah*)." Matthew, a former tax collector, was one of the twelve apostles and author of the Gospel bearing his name. Matt. 9:9–13; 10:1–4; Mark 3:16–19; Luke 6:12–16; Acts 1:12–13

Melchizedek (King of righteousness)

מַלְכִּי-צֶדֶק mahl-kee-TSEH-dehk

From *melek* ("king") and *tsedeq* ("righteousness"). This king of Salem and priest of God Most High is a mysterious figure with no recorded genealogy. Jesus is described as a priest in the order of Melchizedek (Heb. 7:11–17), emphasizing his eternal role as king and priest. Gen. 14:17–20; Ps. 110:4

Micah (Who is like the Lord?)

מִיכָה mee-KHAH

A contraction of the Hebrew name Micayah (*mi/kha/Yah*, "who/is like/the Lord"). The prophet Micah spoke of God's coming judgment and future restoration of his people. Judg. 17:1–18:31; 2 Chron. 18:7–27; Neh. 12:40–43; Jer. 26:17–18; Mic. 1:1

Michael (Who is like God?)

מִיכָאֵל mee-khah-AYL

The meaning of Michael and Micah are nearly the same; the difference is that Michael uses a more general title for God—*El*—rather than *Yah*, the shortened form of his personal name. 1 Chron. 5:11–14; 7:1–3; Dan. 10:1–14; 12:1

Moses (Drawn out)

מֹשֶׁה moh-SHEH

This name sounds like the word *mashah* ("to draw out/pull out"). Pharaoh's daughter drew Moses out of the Nile River when she discovered the basket where his mother had hidden him. Ex. 2:1–3:22; 14:1–15:18; 34:29–35; Num. 20:1–13; Deut. 34:1–12

Joshua (The Lord saves)

יְהוֹשׁוּעַ yuh-hoh-SHOO-ah

The successor to Moses, Joshua led the Israelites into the promised land. His name was originally Hoshea ("he saves"), but Moses renamed him Joshua—"the Lord (*Yah*) saves (*yasha*)". Ex. 17:8–16; Num. 13:1–16; 27:12–23; Josh. 1:1–9; 24:1–31

Josiah (The Lord supports)

יֹאשִׁיָּהוּ yoh-shee-YAH-hoo

A combination of God's shortened personal name, *Yah*, and *oshyah* ("support/foundation"). As a young king, Josiah led the people of Judah back to the Lord as their foundation. 1 Kings 13:1–2; 2 Kings 21:24–22:13; 23:1–30; Jer. 1:2–3

Judah (Praised)

יְהוּדָה yuh-hoo-DAH

Leah named her fourth son Judah to express "praise" (*yadah*) to the Lord. The Greek biblical names Judas and Jude are derived from Judah. Gen. 29:35; 38:1–26; 49:1, 8–12; Deut. 33:1, 7; Josh. 15:1–12

Lazarus (God has helped)

Λάζαρος LAD-zar-os

The Greek form of the Hebrew name Eleazar. The brother of Mary and Martha went by this name, which is fitting since Jesus raised him back to life after he had been dead four days. John 11:1–44; 12:1–11

Leah (Weary?)

לֵאָה lay-AH

The root word is likely *lahah* ("to weary"). Leah carried the wearying burden of competing with her sister, Rachel, for Jacob's affection. Gen. 29:16–35; 30:9–21; 46:8–15; 49:31

Levi (Joined)

לֵוִי lay-VEE

At Levi's birth, Leah declared that her husband, Jacob, would "join" (*lavah*), or connect to her because she had now borne him three sons. Gen. 29:34; 34:1–31; 49:1, 5–7; Deut. 10:8–9; 33:1, 8–11

Luke (Light-giving)

Λουκᾶς loo-KAS

An abbreviated version of the name Lucanus, based on the Latin root *lux* ("light"). Luke authored the Gospel of Luke and the book of Acts. Philem. 1:23–24; 2 Tim. 4:11; Col. 4:14

Malachi (My messenger)

מַלְאָכִי mahl-ah-KHEE

Little is known about this prophet. Malachi is either his proper name or a pseudonym, symbolizing his role as a messenger (*malakh*) speaking the word of the Lord. Mal. 1:1

Manasseh (Causing to forget)

מְנַשֶּׁה muh-nahsh-SHEH

Joseph named his first son Manasseh to commemorate how God had reversed his plight, causing him to forget (*nashah*) all the hardship he had experienced. Gen. 41:50–51; 48:1–22; Deut. 33:1, 13–17; Josh. 17:1–18

Mark (A defense/warlike)

Μᾶρκος MAR-kos

Mark has Latin origins related to Mars, a mythical war figure. Like many men of his time, John Mark, author of the Gospel of Mark, had both a Hebrew name (John) and a Roman name (Mark). Acts 12:12; 15:36–40; Philem. 1:23–24; 2 Tim. 4:11; 1 Pet. 5:13

Job (Persecuted? He who turns?)

אִיּוֹב ee-YOHV

If Hebrew in origin, Job may mean "persecuted" or "enemy." If Arabic, it may mean "he who turns," in the sense of "he who is repentant." Considering the details of Job's suffering and his response to God's speech from the whirlwind, aspects of both meanings are fitting. Job 1:1–2:10; 42:7–17

Joel (The LORD is God)

יוֹאֵל yoh-AYL

The prophet Joel urged the people of Judah to repent and return to the truth that only Yahweh is God. His name combines *El* and a shortened form of *Yahweh*, two of the most common names of God. Joel 1:1

John (The LORD is gracious)

Ἰωάννης ee-oh-AN-nayce

A Greek name derived from the Hebrew name Yochanan, combining *Yah* (short for *Yahweh*) and *khanan* ("to be gracious"). Several men in the Bible have this name, most prominently John the Baptist and John the apostle. Matt. 4:21–22; 10:2–4; 11:11–12; Luke 1:8–20; Acts 12:11–12

Jonathan (The LORD has given)

יְהוֹנָתָן yuh-hoh-nah-TAHN

Combines *natan* ("to give") with God's personal name, *Yahweh*. God gave King Saul's son Jonathan to David as a cherished friend. 1 Sam. 14:1–14; 18:1–4; 20:1–42; 2 Sam. 1:1–27; 9:1–7

Jonah (Dove)

יוֹנָה yoh-NAH

This fleeing prophet's name means "dove" or "pigeon"—one of many biblical names derived from the name of an animal. 2 Kings 14:23–25; Jonah 1:1–3; 2:1–3:4; 3:10–4:11

Joseph (May he add)

יוֹסֵף yoh-SAYF

From the root word *yasaf* ("to increase"). Rachel named her firstborn son Joseph, expressing her desire for another son. God granted her request with the birth of Benjamin. Gen. 30:22–24; 35:16–18; 37:2–28; 39:1–50:26; Deut. 33:1, 13–17

ROSE PUBLISHING

Published by Rose Publishing
an imprint of Tyndale House Ministries

rose-publishing.com

Printed in the United States of America. 010625EPI

Cover photo by shutterstock.com/g/korkeng

Contributing authors: Madison C. Cannon, ThM, and Anisa Larramore

RELIGION / Biblical Reference / Language Study

ISBN: 978-1-4964-9049-0

9 781496 490490

90490 *Biblical Names and Their Meanings*